NATIONAL SECURITY STRATEGY
of the United States

Also available from Brassey's:

NATIONAL SECURITY STRATEGY OF THE
UNITED STATES
by Ronald Reagan (1988)

NATIONAL SECURITY STRATEGY OF THE
UNITED STATES: 1990–1991
by George Bush (1990)

NATIONAL SECURITY STRATEGY
of the United States:
1991-1992

GEORGE BUSH

BRASSEY'S (US), Inc.
A Division of Maxwell Macmillan, Inc.

WASHINGTON • NEW YORK • LONDON • OXFORD • BEIJING
FRANKFURT • SÃO PAULO • SYDNEY • TOKYO • TORONTO

First Edition 1991
BRASSEY'S (US), INC.

Editorial Offices
Brassey's (US), Inc.
8000 Westpark Drive
First Floor
McLean, Virginia 22102

Order Department
Brassey's Book Orders
c/o Macmillan Publishing Co.
100 Front Street, Box 500
Riverside, New Jersey 08075

Brassey's (US), Inc., books are available at special discounts for bulk purchases for sales promotions, premiums, fund-raising, or educational use through the Special Sales Director, Macmillan Publishing Company, 866 Third Avenue, New York, NY 10022.

Library of Congress Cataloging-in-Publication Data
United States. President (1989– : Bush)
National security strategy of the United States : 1991–1992 / George Bush.—1st ed.
  p. cm.
 ISBN 0-08-040578-9.
 1. United States—Foreign relations—1989– 2. United States—National security. I. Bush, George, 1924– .
II. Title.
E881.U55 1991
327.73—dc20
                                                                91-33646
                                                                    CIP

10 9 8 7 6 5 4 3 2 1
Printed in the United States of America

Publisher's Note

The *National Security Strategy of the United States* is the President's articulation to the U.S. Congress of American strategic objectives. Brassey's is pleased to publish this public document to ensure that it is broadly available to American citizens, who remain vitally interested in our nation's role in the world.

Franklin D. Margiotta, Ph.D.

President and Publisher
Brassey's (US), Inc.

An AUSA Book

The Association of the United States Army, or AUSA, was founded in 1950 as a not-for-profit organization dedicated to education concerning the role of the U.S. Army, to providing material for military professional development, and to the promotion of proper recognition and appreciation of the profession of arms. Its constituencies include those who serve in the Army today, including Army National Guard, Army Reserve, and Army civilians, and the retirees and veterans who have served in the past, and all their families. A large number of public-minded citizens and business leaders are also an important constituency. The Association seeks to educate the public, elected and appointed officials, and leaders of defense industry on crucial issues involving the adequacy of our national defense, particularly those issues affecting land warfare.

In 1988 AUSA established within its existing organization a new entity known as the Institute of Land Warfare. Its purpose is to extend the educational work of AUSA by sponsoring scholarly publications, to include books, monographs, and essays on key defense issues, as well as workshops and symposia. Among the volumes chosen for designation as "An AUSA Institute of Land Warfare Book" are both new texts and reprints of titles of enduring value that are no longer in print. Topics include history, policy issues, strategy, and tactics. Publication as an AUSA Book does not indicate that the Association of the United States Army and the publisher agree with everything in the book, but does suggest that the AUSA and the publisher believe this book will stimulate the thinking of AUSA members and others concerned about important issues.

Contents

Preface   xiii

I. The Foundations of National Strategy: Interests and Goals   1

New Era   3
Our Interests and Objectives in the 1990s   11

II. Trends in the World Today: New Opportunities and Concerns   17

Fundamental Transformations   19
    The Soviet Future   19
    The Growing Roles of Germany and Japan   23
    The New Europe   25
Regional Trends   30
    The Western Hemisphere   32
    East Asia and the Pacific   36
    The Middle East and South Asia   40
    Africa   44

III. Relating Means to Ends: A Political Agenda for the 1990s   47

Alliances, Coalitions and a New United Nations   49

The Contest of Ideas and the Nurturing of Democracy	52
Arms Control	53
Stemming Proliferation	58
Intelligence Programs	63
Economic and Security Assistance	65
Illicit Drugs	67
Immigrants and Refugees	70

IV. Relating Means to Ends: An Economic Agenda for the 1990s — 73

Economic Challenges	75
Maintaining Economic Growth	77
Global Imbalances	78
Debt	79
Trade	81
Technology	83
Energy	85
The Environment	88
Space	89

V. Relating Means to Ends: A Defense Agenda for the 1990s — 95

Nuclear Deterrence	98
Strategic Nuclear Forces	*99*
Non-Strategic Nuclear Forces	*103*
Missile Defenses	*104*

Forward Presence	107
Across the Atlantic: Europe and the Middle East	*108*
Across the Pacific	*110*
The Rest of the World	*112*
Crisis Response	112
Mobility	*114*
Readiness and Our Guard and Reserve Forces	*115*
Reconstitution	118
Manpower	*119*
Defense Technology	*120*
The Industrial Base	*122*
A Smaller and Restructured Force	124
Minimum Essential Military Forces—	
The Base Force	*124*

VI. Toward the 21st Century — 129

Preface

A New World Order

A new world order is not a fact; it is an aspiration—and an opportunity. We have within our grasp an extraordinary possibility that few generations have enjoyed—to build a new international system in accordance with our own values and ideals, as old patterns and certainties crumble around us.

In the Gulf we caught a glimmer of a better future—a new world community brought together by a growing consensus that force cannot be used to settle disputes and that when that consensus is broken, the world will respond. In the Gulf, we saw the United Nations playing the role dreamed of by its founders, with the world's leading nations orchestrating and sanctioning collective action against aggression. But we remain in a period of transition. The old has been swept away, the new not yet fully in place. The obstacles and uncertainties before us are quite real—

the daunting problems confronting the hopes for reform in Eastern Europe and the Soviet Union, trade disputes and burdensharing debates among the industrial democracies, and the turmoil and dangers in the developing world.

Yet, the Gulf crisis showed what the world community is now capable of, and in the very act of meeting that challenge the world community strengthened itself. I hope history will record that the Gulf crisis was the crucible of the new world order.

It is up to us—our generation in America and the world—to bring these extraordinary possibilities to fruition. And in doing this, American leadership is indispensable. That is our challenge.

Our response, outlined in this Report, is shaped by what we are as a people, for our values are the link between our past and our future, between our domestic life and our foreign policy, between our power and our purpose. It is our deepest belief that all nations and peoples seek political and economic freedom; that governments must rest their rightful authority on the consent of the governed, and must live in peace with their neighbors. The collapse of the Communist idea has shown that our vision of individual rights—a vision imbedded in the faith of our Founders—speaks to humanity's enduring hopes and aspirations.

It is this abiding faith in democracy that steels us to deal with a world that, for all our hope, remains a dangerous place—a world of ethnic antagonisms, national rivalries, religious tensions, spreading weaponry, personal ambitions and lingering authoritarianism. For America, there can be no retreat from the world's problems. Within the broader community of nations, we see our own role clearly. We must not only protect our citizens and our interests, but help create a new world in which our fundamental values not only survive but flourish. We must work with others, but we must also be a leader.

·I·
THE FOUNDATIONS OF NATIONAL STRATEGY:
Interests and Goals

New Era

The bitter struggle that divided the world for over two generations has come to an end. The collapse of Soviet domination in Eastern Europe means that the Cold War is over, its core issue resolved. We have entered a new era, one whose outline would have been unimaginable only three years ago.

This new era offers great hope, but this hope must be tempered by the even greater uncertainty we face. Almost immediately new crises and instabilities came upon us. The Gulf War was a forceful reminder that there are still autonomous sources of turbulence in the world. In the Soviet Union, while we have seen a healthy retrenchment in foreign policy, we also see a continuing internal crisis, with a danger of violence overhanging the hopes for internal reform. We face new challenges not only to our security, but to our ways of thinking about security.

For over 40 years, the American grand strategy of containment has reflected an era of expanding Soviet power, Soviet aggression and Soviet Communism. We now find, however, that the Soviet Union is far more inwardly focused as it wrestles with its internal crises. We do not know what path the Soviet Union will ultimately take, but a return to the same superpower adversary we have faced for over 40 years is unlikely.

That said, the Soviet Union remains the only state possessing the physical military capability to destroy American society with a single, cataclysmic attack and, in spite of severe economic strains, the modernization of Soviet strategic forces continues virtually across the board. Even with a START Treaty, the Soviets will retain more than 6,000 strategic weapons. The Soviets will also—despite the heartening reductions we have seen in their conventional capabilities—retain some three million men in their armed forces. These enduring realities cannot be ignored.

Shaping a security strategy for a new era will require an understanding of the extraordinary trends at work today—a clear picture of what has changed and what has not, an accurate sense of the opportunities that history has put before us and a sober appreciation of the dangers that remain.

Politically, a key issue is how America's role of alliance leader—and indeed our alliances themselves—will be affected, especially in Europe, by a reduced Soviet threat. The positive common basis of our alliances—the defense of democratic values—must be reaffirmed and strengthened. Yet, differences among allies are likely to become more evident as the traditional concern for security that first brought them together diminishes in intensity. We need to consider how the United States and its allies can best respond to a new agenda of political challenges—such as the troubled evolution of the Soviet Union or the volatile Middle East—in the framework of the moral and political values we continue to share.

In the realm of *military* strategy, we confront dangers more ambiguous than those we previously faced. What type and distribution of forces are needed to combat not a particular, poised enemy but the nascent threats of power vacuums and regional instabilities? How do we reduce our conventional capabilities in ways that ensure we could rebuild them faster than an enemy could build a devastating new threat against us? How does the proliferation of advanced weaponry affect our traditional problem of deterrence? How should we think about these new military challenges and what capabilities and forces should we develop to secure ourselves against them?

America will continue to support an international *economic* system as open and inclusive as possible, as the best way to strengthen global economic development, political stability and the growth of free societies. But how can these goals best be attained, especially if they are not completely shared by all of our economic competitors? How will the end of the Cold War and the increased economic strength of our major trading partners influence economic, political and even security relationships? In addition to working actively to conclude successfully the Uruguay Round of Multilateral Trade Negotiations, what other market-opening objectives should the

United States pursue, and with whom should we pursue them?

In the emerging post-Cold War world, international relations promise to be more complicated, more volatile and less predictable. Indeed, of all the mistakes that could be made about the security challenges of a new era, the most dangerous would be to believe that suddenly the future can be predicted with certainty. The history of the 20th century has been replete with surprises, many unwelcome.

In many ways, if there is a historical analogy for today's strategic environment, it is less the late 1940s than it is the 1920s. In the 1920s, judging that the great threat to our interests had collapsed and that no comparable threat was evident, the Nation turned inward. That course had near disastrous consequences then and it would be even more dangerous now. At a time when the world is far more interdependent—economically, technologically, environmentally—any attempt to isolate ourselves militarily and politically would be folly.

Despite the emergence of new power centers, the United States remains the only state with truly global strength, reach and influence in every dimension—political, economic and military. In these circumstances, our natural desire to share burdens more equitably with newly-strong friends does not relieve us of our own responsibilities.

America's role is rooted not only in power, but also in trust. When, in the aftermath of the invasion of Kuwait, the Saudis invited foreign forces onto their soil, King Fahd observed:

> *I trust the United States of America. I know that when you say you will be committed, you are, in fact, committed. I know that you will stay as long as necessary to do what has to be done, and I know you will leave when you are asked to leave at the end, and that you have no ulterior motives.*

We cannot be the world's policeman with responsibility for solving all the world's security problems. But we remain the country to whom others turn when in distress. This faith in us creates burdens, certainly, and in the Gulf we showed that American leadership must include mobilizing the world community to share the danger and risk. But the failure of others to bear their burden would not excuse us. In the end, we are answerable to our own interests and our own conscience—to our ideals and to history—for what we do with the power we have. In the 1990s, as for much of this century, there is no substitute for American leadership. Our responsibility, even in a new era, is pivotal and inescapable.

The Gulf crisis interrupted a time of hope. We saw a new world coming, a world freer from the threat of terror, stronger in the pursuit of justice, more secure in the quest for peace. Democracy was gaining ground as were the principles of human rights and political and economic freedom. This new world is still within reach, perhaps brought closer by the unprecedented international cooperation achieved in the Gulf crisis.

But even after such a success, we face not only the complex security issues outlined above, but a new agenda of new kinds of security issues. Our national power, for example, ultimately rests on the strength and resilience of our economy, and our security would be badly served if we allowed fiscal irresponsibility at home to erode our ability to protect our interests abroad, to aid new democracies or to help find solutions to other global problems. The scourge of illegal drugs saps our vitality as a free people, diverts our energies from more positive pursuits and threatens friendly democratic governments now plagued by drug traffickers. The environmental depredations of Saddam Hussein have underscored that protecting the global ecology is a top priority on the agenda of international cooperation—from extinguishing oil fires in Kuwait to preserving the rain forests to solving water disputes to assessing climate change. The upheavals of this era are also giving rise to human migrations on an unprecedented scale, raising a host of social, economic, political and moral challenges to the world's nations.

A security strategy that takes the Republic safely into the next century will tend to these as well as to more traditional threats to our safety and well-being.

Our Interests and Objectives in the 1990s

We need, then, an approach to security broad enough to preserve the basic sources of our national strength and focused enough to deal with the very real threats that still exist. Such an approach begins with an understanding of our basic interests and objectives, interests and objectives that even in a new era are enduring:

The survival of the United States as a free and independent nation, with its fundamental values intact and its institutions and people secure.

The United States seeks, whenever possible in concert with its allies, to:

- deter any aggression that could threaten the security of the United States and its allies and—should deterrence fail—repel or defeat military attack and end conflict on terms favorable to the United States, its interests and its allies;

- effectively counter threats to the security of the United States and its citizens and interests short of armed conflict, including the threat of international terrorism;

- improve stability by pursuing equitable and verifiable arms control agreements, modernizing our strategic deterrent, developing systems capable of defending against limited ballistic-missile strikes, and enhancing appropriate conventional capabilities;

- promote democratic change in the Soviet Union, while maintaining firm policies that discourage any temptation to new quests for military advantage;

- foster restraint in global military spending and discourage military adventurism;

- prevent the transfer of militarily critical technologies and resources to hostile countries or groups, especially the spread of chemical, biological and nuclear weapons and associated high-technology means of delivery; and

- reduce the flow of illegal drugs into the United States by encouraging reduction in foreign production, combatting the international traffickers and reducing demand at home.

A healthy and growing U.S. economy to ensure opportunity for individual prosperity and resources for national endeavors at home and abroad.

National security and economic strength are indivisible. We seek to:

- promote a strong, prosperous and competitive U.S. economy;
- ensure access to foreign markets, energy, mineral resources, the oceans and space;

- promote an open and expanding international economic system, based on market principles, with minimal distortions to trade and investment, stable currencies, and broadly respected rules for managing and resolving economic disputes; and
- achieve cooperative international solutions to key environmental challenges, assuring the sustainability and environmental security of the planet as well as growth and opportunity for all.

Healthy, cooperative and politically vigorous relations with allies and friendly nations.

To build and sustain such relationships, we seek to:

- strengthen and enlarge the commonwealth of free nations that share a commitment to democracy and individual rights;
- establish a more balanced partnership with our allies and a greater sharing of global leadership and responsibilities;

- strengthen international institutions like the United Nations to make them more effective in promoting peace, world order and political, economic and social progress;

- support Western Europe's historic march toward greater economic and political unity, including a European security identity within the Atlantic Alliance, and nurture a closer relationship between the United States and the European Community; and

- work with our North Atlantic allies to help develop the processes of the Conference on Security and Cooperation in Europe to bring about reconciliation, security and democracy in a Europe whole and free.

A stable and secure world, where political and economic freedom, human rights and democratic institutions flourish.

Our interests are best served in a world in which democracy and its ideals are widespread and secure. We seek to:

- maintain stable regional military balances to deter those powers that might seek regional dominance;
- promote diplomatic solutions to regional disputes;
- promote the growth of free, democratic political institutions as the surest guarantors of both human rights and economic and social progress;
- aid in combatting threats to democratic institutions from aggression, coercion, insurgencies, subversion, terrorism and illicit drug trafficking; and
- support aid, trade and investment policies that promote economic development and social and political progress.

·II·
TRENDS IN THE WORLD TODAY: New Opportunities and Concerns

Fundamental Transformations

Despite the uncertainties that remain, we see a fundamental transformation of the global strategic environment in several areas. Our policies and strategy for the decade ahead must be designed to adapt to these changes, and to shape them in ways that benefit the United States and its friends and allies.

The Soviet Future

If Central and Eastern Europe was the scene of the peaceful Revolution of 1989, the dramatic story of 1991 is the deepening crisis within the Soviet Union. The old system of Communist orthodoxy is discredited, yet its diehard adherents have not given up the struggle against change. Fundamental choices—of multi-party democracy, national self-determination and market economic reform—have been postponed too long. The economy is deteriorating. The painful process of establishing new, legitimate political and economic institutions has much farther to go.

If reform is to succeed, Soviet leaders must move decisively to effect institutional change. When invited and where appropriate, we will offer our cooperation. But it is clearly not in our interest to offer assistance in a way that allows the Soviet government to avoid the hard choices that in the longer run are the only hope for the people of that country. At the July 1991 London Economic Summit, the participants announced their support for special associate status for the Soviet Union in the IMF and World Bank. This will give the Soviets access to the technical advice they need to formulate and implement their reform program.

The processes of reform inside the Soviet Union have already had a revolutionary impact on Soviet foreign policy. With former ideological imperatives giving way to a new pragmatism, areas of cooperation have expanded. The end of Soviet domination of Eastern Europe was a transforming event. Soviet policy toward the unification of Germany was constructive. The reduced role of ideology in Soviet foreign policy has diminished the importance of many developing areas as arenas of conflict with the West. Soviet support in the UN Security Council for the resolutions against Iraqi aggression was an important contribution to the international effort. We are hopeful that such cooperation can be expanded. Of course, the Soviets would pay a severe political price for any return to practices of an earlier era, exploiting regional disputes and instabilities for their presumed advantage.

Today, the threat of a U.S.-Soviet military conflict is lower than at any time since the end of World War II. With the ongoing withdrawal of Soviet forces from Eastern Europe, the unilateral reductions now underway and the recently signed CFE treaty (if faithfully implemented), the threat of a sudden, massive offensive against NATO will have been eliminated. Despite uncertainty over the Soviet internal evolution, any attempt by the Soviets to restore such a threat would require lengthy preparation and be enormously costly and virtually impossible to conceal. Moreover, the START Treaty signed at the

Moscow Summit will significantly reduce U.S. and Soviet strategic nuclear arsenals.

But Soviet military power is hardly becoming irrelevant. The Soviet Union is and will remain a military superpower. Beyond its modernized strategic arsenal, the Soviet Union's conventional forces west of the Urals will dwarf any other national force in Europe. While they no longer pose the threat of a short-warning, theater-wide offensive, they could still pose a potent threat to a single flank or region. The size and orientation of Soviet military forces must therefore remain critical concerns to the United States and the overall health of the European system will still require a counterweight to Soviet military strength.

It is our responsibility as a government to hedge against the uncertainties of the future. Elements of the U.S.-Soviet relationship will remain competitive, and there is always the danger that confrontations will re-emerge. Our evolving relationship is also not immune to Soviet attempts to lay the problems created by decades of domestic tyranny, misrule and mismanagement at the feet of "foreign enemies." Nor is it immune to the implications of the forceful repression of democratic forces, slowing the Soviet Union's progress on a road that must be taken if it is to successfully meet the challenges before it. The internal order of a state is ultimately reflected in its external behavior. We will remain alert to the potential strategic consequences of a return to totalitarian policies.

The Growing Roles of Germany and Japan

One of the most important and far-reaching strategic developments of a new era—and a major success of America's postwar policy—is the emergence of Japan and Germany as economic and political leaders. The United States has long encouraged such a development, and our close ties with these democracies have created the climate of reassurance necessary for their evolution as stable and powerful countries enjoying good relations with their neighbors. As these countries assume a greater political role, the health of

American ties with them—political, military and economic—will remain crucial to regional and even global stability. These links are not relics of an earlier period. They are all the more needed in a new era as these countries' roles expand.

But we frequently find ourselves competitors—sometimes even bitter competitors—in the economic arena. These frictions must be managed if we are to preserve the partnerships that have fostered reconciliation, reassurance, democracy and security in the postwar period. In this sense, ongoing trade negotiations now share some of the strategic importance we have traditionally attached to arms talks with the Soviet Union.

The Gulf crisis has also reopened, with a new sense of urgency, the question of responsibility-sharing—not only with respect to sharing the costs and risks of Gulf operations, but also with regard to sharing the costs of U.S. forces defending Europe and Japan. Our allies are doing more, as befits their economic strength, but the issue may grow more acute as we and they adjust to a new era.

The New Europe

It is Europe more than any other area that has held the key to the global balance in this century, and it is this continent more than any other that is experiencing fundamental change. The unification of Germany last October quickened the pace to a new, more promising era and a continent truly whole and free. As Europe is being transformed politically, we are also lifting the military shadows and fears with which we have lived for nearly half a century.

All across the Continent, the barriers that once confined people and ideas are collapsing. East Europeans are determining their own destinies, choosing freedom and economic liberty. One by one, the states of Central and Eastern Europe have begun to reclaim the European cultural and political tradition that is their heritage. All Soviet forces are gone from Czechoslovakia and Hungary and withdrawals from Germany and Poland are underway. The military capability of the Soviet forces still remaining in Eastern Europe is rapidly diminishing and the Warsaw Pact has been dissolved.

Basic to the new structure of peace we seek to build throughout Europe is the continued vitality of the North Atlantic Alliance—the indispensable foundation of transatlantic cooperation. To keep the Alliance strong and viable in a new environment we must recognize that there are important tasks beyond the changed—but still important—requirement to balance and deter Soviet military power. NATO must deter and defend against the threat of aggression from any state against the territory of a NATO member. NATO will also be essential in promoting a stable security environment throughout Europe, an environment based on democratic institutions and the peaceful resolution of disputes, an environment free of intimidation or attempts at hegemony. Finally, NATO still serves as an indispensable transatlantic forum for consultations on issues that affect common political and security interests.

As the European Community heads toward the new milestone of a single market by the end of

1992, we enter a revolution of relations in the West, perhaps ultimately as important strategically as the revolution taking place in the East. It is no accident that Europeans are contemplating greater West European cohesion in the security field, even while preserving the vital transatlantic framework. We will work to adapt NATO's structures to encompass European desires for a distinct security identity within the Alliance and we will encourage greater European responsibility for Europe's defense. While European governments will naturally take the lead in developing their own institutions, these efforts will enjoy our full support as long as they strengthen the Alliance. We will also work to adapt Alliance command structures to new realities—the reassessment of risks, a new NATO strategy, a different force structure—in ways that sustain the unique contribution of NATO's integrated military command.

The continued freedom, vitality and national independence of the new Eastern European democracies are also critical to the new structure of peace we seek to build throughout Europe. Any reversal of the present positive trend in Soviet policy would have serious implications. As the North Atlantic allies declared in June: "Our own security is inseparably linked to that of all other states in Europe. The consolidation and preservation throughout the continent of democratic societies and their freedom from any form of coercion or intimidation are therefore of direct and material concern to us." We and our NATO allies have established a program of contacts with the militaries of these states to support military establishments that will sustain newly won freedoms and we have extended our bilateral International Military Education and Training (IMET) program to strengthen the military professionalism and to promote the principle of civilian oversight of the armed forces.

It is important that we not let euphoria over the easing of East-West confrontation blind us to the potential security problems within a new Europe. Historical enmities in Western Europe have been largely consigned to the past but disputes between and among some East European states and ethnic groups appear to have been merely frozen in time by decades of Cold War. In the interwar period, the politics of these states were often dominated by economic hardship, competing nationalisms and overlapping territorial claims. We have reason to be more hopeful today, but security problems could emerge in the East in the course of the 1990s. The powerful centrifugal forces in Yugoslavia are particularly worrisome.

The overall structure of peace in Europe must be made solid enough to withstand the turmoil that looms ahead. We need to develop the processes and principles of the Conference on Security and Cooperation in Europe (CSCE) and perhaps other mechanisms to ease ethnic and national tensions and to dampen and resolve conflicts.

Europe also may be about to face a new problem, not new in kind, but in scope: mass migrations and flows of refugees in response to the breakdown of the communist world and the magnetic attraction of Western European prosperity. From the Soviet Union and Eastern Europe, from North Africa and the Near East, we could see thousands fleeing economic hardship and seeking a better life. For Western European countries, there could be enormous economic, social and political strains—an unprecedented challenge to the new Europe, testing its moral and political character.

Regional Trends

While Europe remains a central strategic arena, the Gulf crisis reminded us how much our interests can be affected in other regions as well.

As the effects of the Cold War recede, regional disputes are less likely automatically to be perceived as part of a permanent—frequently dangerous, sometimes violent—global competition, thus allowing broader international cooperation in their resolution.

Less happily, in some regions this overall positive trend could unleash local, destructive forces that were formerly kept in check. As we saw in the Gulf, there is the danger of locally dominant powers, armed with modern weaponry and ancient ambitions, threatening the world's hope for a new era of cooperation. We see regimes that have made themselves champions of regional radicalism, states that are all too vulnerable to such pressures, governments that refuse to recognize one another, and countries that have claims on one another's territory—some with significant military capabilities and a history of recurring war. A key task for the future will be maintaining regional balances and resolving such disputes before they erupt in military conflict.

If the end of the Cold War lives up to its promise and liberates U.S. policy from many of its earlier concerns, we should be able to concentrate more on enhancing security—in the developing world, particularly—through means that are more political, social and economic than military. We must recognize the stark fact that our hopeful new era still has within it dislocations and dangers that threaten the fragile shoots of democracy and progress that have recently emerged. Malnutrition, illiteracy and poverty put dangerous pressures on democratic institutions as hungry, uneducated or poorly housed citizens are ripe for radicalization by movements of the left and the right. Our response to need and turmoil must increasingly emphasize the strengthening of democracy, and a long-term investment in the development of human resources and the structures of free markets and free governments. Such measures are an investment in our own security as well as a response to the demands of simple justice.

The Western Hemisphere

Nowhere is this more true than in our own hemisphere, where our fundamental aims are to deepen the sense of partnership and common interest.

Latin Americans have long argued that U.S. interest has waxed and waned with the rise and fall of extra-hemispheric threats to regional security. Our policy has sought to allay these fears, as it is founded on the principle of a common destiny and mutual responsibility. The Western

Hemisphere is all the more significant to the United States in light of today's global trends, political and economic.

The resurgence of democracy, the worldwide phenomenon that is such an inspiration to us, is heading toward a dramatic achievement—a completely democratic hemisphere. This drive gained momentum last year with the election of democratic governments in Nicaragua and Haiti, the restoration of democracy in Panama, and several other democratic elections. The electoral defeat of the Sandinista government in Nicaragua is especially noteworthy as it has led to the end of Soviet and Cuban military assistance, thereby increasing the security of all of Central America. The United States has provided political and economic support for the new government and its program for reconstruction and long-term development. Despite these successes, we realize that democratic institutions in much of Latin America remain fragile, and we are seeking ways to strengthen them.

In our military-to-military relations, we will continue to promote professionalism, support for civilian authority and respect for human rights. With recent legislative changes, we can more easily include civilian officials in our IMET program. Effective civilian control of the military will become a reality only when there is a cadre of competent civilian resource managers with the expertise to take the lead in defense issues.

Cuba remains a holdout in the hemisphere's transition to democracy but it is simply a matter of time before fundamental change occurs there, too. We will continue to press the Soviet Union to reduce its aid and presence in Cuba and we will enlist our friends in the hemisphere in pressing Cuba to accept the inevitable peacefully. In Central America, we support the regional trend toward negotiation, demilitarization and demobilization. The nations most severely threatened by guerrilla forces or narco-terrorists—El Salvador, Colombia and Peru—will receive appropriate support from the United States.

As many countries make the transition to democracy, a strong tide of economic realism and dedication to market-oriented reforms is also sweeping the region. Our interest in supporting both democratic and economic transitions in Latin America and the Caribbean is demonstrated by the new Enterprise for the Americas Initiative. This Initiative, which has been warmly welcomed in the region, sets out a vision of hemispheric prosperity achieved through expanded trade, increased investment, reduced debt burdens and important support for protection of the hemisphere's vital natural heritage. Concrete steps have been taken toward a hemispheric free trade area, including work on trade and investment framework agreements and a Free Trade Agreement embracing both Mexico and Canada. We are also encouraging countries to take steps to compete for capital and are working to reduce bilateral official debt of countries committed to strong economic reforms. We are seeking prompt Congressional approval of enabling legislation. In addition, we have proposed a specific trade preference system (patterned after the successful Caribbean Basin Initiative) to help Andean countries break out of their dependence on illegal drug crops. We will also work with our friends to develop the initiatives that make up the Partnership for Democracy and Development in Central America.

East Asia and the Pacific

East Asia and the Pacific are home to some of the world's most economically and politically dynamic societies. The region also includes some of the last traditional Communist regimes on the face of the globe. Regional hotspots tragically persist on the Korean peninsula and in Cambodia, and there are territorial disputes in which progress is long overdue, including the Soviet Union's continued occupation of Japan's Northern Territories.

In this complex environment, an era of Soviet adventurism is on the ebb, even while its effects linger. This is placing new stresses on Vietnam, Cambodia and North Korea as Soviet military and economic aid declines and Moscow seeks to improve relations with Seoul, Tokyo and other capitals. China is coming to view its neighbors in a new light, and is gradually adjusting to a changing perception of the Soviet threat.

Through a web of bilateral relationships, the United States has pursued throughout the postwar period a policy of engagement in support of the stability and security that are prerequisites to economic and political progress. U.S. power remains welcome in key states in the region, who recognize the pivotal role we continue to play in the regional balance. We remain a key factor of reassurance and stability. By ensuring freedom of the seas through naval and air strength and by offering these capabilities as a counterweight in the region's power equations, we are likely to remain welcome in an era of shifting patterns and possible new frictions.

Today's basically healthy conditions cannot be taken for granted. We will continue to be a beacon for democracy and human rights. We will meet our responsibilities in the security field. We will also remain actively engaged in promoting free and expanding markets through Asian Pacific Economic Cooperation, recognizing that economic progress is a major ingredient in Asia's political stability and democratic progress.

As noted earlier, our alliance with Japan remains of enormous strategic importance. Our hope is to see the U.S.-Japan global partnership extend beyond its traditional confines and into fields like refugee relief, non-proliferation and the environment.

On the Korean peninsula, we and the Republic of Korea seek to persuade North Korea of the benefit of confidence-building measures as a first step to lasting peace and reunification. We firmly believe that true stability can only be achieved through direct North-South talks. At the same time, the United States remains committed to the security of the Republic of Korea as it continues to open its economic and political systems. We are increasingly concerned about North Korea's failure to observe its obligations under the Nuclear Non-Proliferation Treaty, and consider this to be the most pressing security issue on the peninsula.

China, like the Soviet Union, poses a complex

challenge as it proceeds inexorably toward major systemic change. China's inward focus and struggle to achieve stability will not preclude increasing interaction with its neighbors as trade and technology advance. Consultations and contact with China will be central features of our policy, lest we intensify the isolation that shields repression. Change is inevitable in China, and our links with China must endure.

The United States maintains strong, unofficial, substantive relations with Taiwan where rapid economic and political change is underway. One of our goals is to foster an environment in which Taiwan and the People's Republic of China can pursue a constructive and peaceful interchange across the Taiwan Strait.

In Southeast Asia, there is renewed hope for a settlement in Cambodia. Only through resolution of the conflict in Cambodia can there be the promise of our restoring normal relations with that beleaguered nation and with Vietnam. Hanoi and Phnom Penh have sadly delayed the day when they can enjoy normal ties with us or their Southeast Asian neighbors. Of course, the pace and scope of our actions will also be directly affected by steps that are taken to resolve the fate of Americans still unaccounted for. The resolution of this issue remains one of our highest priorities.

Even with the loss of Clark Air Base, we remain committed to helping the Philippines make a success of its new democracy and to fulfilling our legitimate defense function there as allies and equals. In the South Pacific, we are demonstrating renewed interest in and assistance for the island states. Australia retains its special position as a steadfast ally and key Pacific partner. We look forward to the day when New Zealand will choose to resume its responsibilities to the ANZUS alliance and rejoin Australia and the United States in this important regional structure.

The Middle East and South Asia

The reversal of Iraq's aggression against Kuwait was a watershed event. Nonetheless, our basic policy toward the region shows powerful continuity. American strategic concerns still include promoting stability and the security of our friends, maintaining a free flow of oil, curbing the proliferation of weapons of mass destruction and ballistic missiles, discouraging destabilizing conventional arms sales, countering terrorism and encouraging a peace process that brings about reconciliation between Israel and the Arab states as well as between Palestinians and Israel in a manner consonant with our enduring commitment to Israel's security.

The regional environment since Desert Storm presents new challenges and new opportunities. Even as we provide badly needed relief and protection to refugees, we will work to bring about greater security and a lasting peace.

- We will help states in the Middle East to fashion regional security arrangements that bolster deterrence and encourage the peaceful resolution of disputes.
- We will work with parties inside and outside the region to change the destructive pattern of military competition and proliferation. This will involve confidence-

building and arms control measures as well as more global forms of control over the supply of arms, especially weapons of mass destruction and the means to deliver them.

- We will encourage economic reconstruction and recovery, using the political and economic strengths of the victorious coalition to support economic openness and cooperation. We will also encourage regional states to evolve toward greater political participation and respect for human rights.

- We will continue the effort to bring about a comprehensive peace and true reconciliation between Israel and the Arab states and between Israel and the Palestinians.

- We will continue to demand that Iraq comply fully and unconditionally with all relevant UN resolutions, including Security Council Resolution 687 and its stipulation that Iraqi weapons of mass destruction and ballistic missile-related facilities be destroyed.

- We remain open to an improved relationship with Iran. However, meaningful improvement can only occur after Iran makes clear it is lending no support to hostage-taking or other forms of terrorism.
- We will also continue to monitor Libyan behavior, including terrorism, proliferation of weapons of mass destruction and attempts to destabilize neighboring governments.

In South Asia, as elsewhere, we strongly believe that security is best served by resolving disputes through negotiations rather than military pressure. The dangers of intermediate-range missile deployments and nuclear proliferation in the subcontinent persist, however, and this year we were unable to certify Pakistan's nuclear program under the Pressler Amendment. We will continue to encourage Indo-Pakistani rapprochement and the adoption of confidence-building measures and other concrete steps to moderate their military competition. We also remain committed to achieving a comprehensive political settlement in Afghanistan.

Africa

The end of the Cold War should benefit Africa in that it will no longer be seen as a battleground for superpower conflict. In a world at peace, more attention and resources should be freed to help the world's poorest. Nonetheless, many Africans now fear that the outside world will lose interest in their troubled continent, just at the moment when many negative trends from economic decline to AIDS to environmental degradation are likely to accelerate.

In a continent as diverse as Africa, democracy—as it emerges, reemerges, or begins its development—may take different forms, and its progress will be uneven. But we need not be inhibited in supporting values that have proved universal—political and human rights, democratic limits on the powers of government, judicial independence, free press and free speech. To those who think these goals are out of reach because of Africa's poverty and disparate cultures, we say that democracy remains the political system most open to cultural diversity and most conducive to economic advance. Freedom, in its universal meaning, is Africa's birthright as much as it is anyone else's.

In the economic realm, hope lies in reducing the burden of statism and encouraging indigenous enterprise and human talent, especially in agriculture. The most important steps are those that must be taken by Africans themselves. Concepts of democracy and market economics must be applied in a continent where initially these concepts were rejected because socialism was fashionable. That failed experiment has now run its course, and political elites across Africa are rediscovering basic truths about political and economic freedom as the source of progress. We need to support this growing realism, which recognizes the failures from the past and which has produced pragmatic new leaders ready to move in new directions. Benign neglect will not suffice.

Africa is not without its beacons of hope. The efforts of white and black leaders in South Africa to move that country into a democratic, constitutional, post-apartheid era merit our active support and we have provided it. We have made clear our firm and enthusiastic support for the brave endeavor on which they have embarked.

Elsewhere in Africa, we can be proud of the role we played in bringing to an end civil wars in Angola and Ethiopia. We continue to play an active role in helping to resolve other conflicts such as those in Liberia and Mozambique.

Africa is now entering an age in which it can benefit from past mistakes and build a realistic, self-sustaining future. It is in our interest, for political as well as humanitarian reasons, to help that process.

·III·
RELATING MEANS TO ENDS:
A Political Agenda for the 1990s

Alliances, Coalitions and a New United Nations

Our first priority in foreign policy remains solidarity with our allies and friends. The stable foundation of our security will continue to be a common effort with peoples with whom we share fundamental moral and political values and security interests. Those nations with whom we are bound by alliances will continue to be our closest partners in building a new world order.

As our response to the Gulf crisis demonstrated, our leadership in a new era must also include a broader concept of international community and international diplomacy. If tensions with the Soviet Union continue to ease, we will face more ambiguous—but still serious—challenges. It will be difficult to foresee where future crises will arise. In many cases they will involve states not part of one or another bloc. Increasingly we may find ourselves in situations in which our interests are congruent with those of nations not tied to us by formal treaties. As in the Gulf, we may be acting in hybrid coalitions that include not only traditional allies but also nations with whom we do not have a mature history of diplomatic and military cooperation or, indeed, even a common political or moral outlook. This will require flexibility in our diplomacy and military policy, without losing sight of the fundamental values which that diplomacy and policy are designed to protect and on which they are based. To this end, we are well served to strengthen the role of international organizations like the United Nations.

For over 40 years political differences, bloc politics and demagogic rhetoric have kept the UN from reaching the full potential envisioned by its founders. Now we see the UN beginning to act as it was designed, freed from the superpower antagonisms that often frustrated consensus, less hobbled by the ritualistic anti-Americanism that so often weakened its credibility.

The response of the UN to Iraq's unprovoked aggression against a member state has truly vindicated and rejuvenated the institution. But even before that, the UN had distinguished itself in fostering democratic change in Namibia and Nicaragua. In the near future, we hope to see it play a constructive role in Afghanistan, Cambodia, the Western Sahara, El Salvador and elsewhere, assisting with elections and the return of displaced persons, as well as with peacekeeping.

The role of the UN in improving the human condition and ameliorating human suffering—development, aid to refugees, education, disaster relief—will continue to attract our leadership and resources. High on our agenda for international cooperation are the global challenges posed by illegal drugs, terrorism and degradation of the environment.

The costs of a world organization that can effectively carry out these missions are already significant and will increase as new tasks are undertaken. We have re-stated our intention to pay in full our annual assessments and are now paying arrearages. We intend to complete arrearage payments no later than 1995 and to pay our share of any new peacekeeping requirements. In voluntary funding, we will pay our fair share and encourage others to do the same.

The Contest of Ideas and the Nurturing of Democracy

Recent history has shown how much ideas count. The Cold War was, in its decisive aspect, a war of ideas. But ideas count only when knowledge spreads. In today's evolving political environment, and in the face of the global explosion of information, we must make clear to our friends and potential adversaries what we stand for.

The need for international understanding among different peoples, cultures, religions and forms of government will only grow. In a world without the clear-cut East-West divisions of the past, the flow of ideas and information will take on larger significance as once-isolated countries seek their way toward the international mainstream. Indeed, information access has already achieved global proportions. A truly global community is being formed, vindicating our democratic values.

Through broadcasts, academic and cultural exchanges, press briefings, publications, speakers and conferences, we engage those abroad in a dialogue about who and what we are—to inform foreign audiences about our policies, democratic traditions, pluralistic society and rich academic and cultural diversity. We will increase our efforts to clarify what America has to contribute to the solution of global problems—and to drive home democracy's place in this process.

Arms Control

Arms control is an important component of a balanced strategy to ameliorate the deadly consequences of global tensions as well as to reduce their fundamental causes. Our goal remains agreements that will enhance the security of the United States and its allies while strengthening international stability by:

- reducing military capabilities that could provide incentives to initiate attack;
- enhancing predictability in the size and structure of forces in order to reduce the fear of aggressive intent;
- ensuring confidence in compliance, through effective verification.

Our pursuit of these goals has profited from the recent, positive changes in East-West relations. With renewed commitment to conscientious implementation and the resolution of remaining issues, we are within reach of completing an arms control agenda that few imagined possible.

Much has already been accomplished. Within the past year we and the Soviets have agreed to cease production of chemical weapons and to destroy, using safe and environmentally-sound procedures, the vast majority of our chemical weapons stocks. We have agreed to new protocols to treaties on limiting underground nuclear weapons tests and nuclear explosions for peaceful purposes, incorporating unprecedented on-site verification of compliance with the limits set by the treaties. At the Paris Summit last November, the United States, the Soviet Union and the other nations of the Conference on Security and Cooperation in Europe (CSCE) endorsed new measures to promote transparency in military dispositions and practices.

Also in Paris, the United States, our North Atlantic allies, the states of Eastern Europe and the Soviet Union signed the Treaty on Conventional Armed Forces in Europe (CFE), a historic agreement that will establish numerical parity in major conventional armaments between East and West from the Atlantic to the Urals. The treaty will require thousands of weapons to be destroyed and includes unprecedented monitoring provisions. Submitting the treaty to the Senate for its advice and consent to ratification was delayed by Soviet claims—made after the treaty was signed—that some of its ground force equipment held by units like naval infantry and coastal defense was not covered by the agreement. The satisfactory resolution of this question has opened the way for us to move forward.

Soviet behavior on CFE complicated the completion of a Strategic Arms Reduction Treaty. However, during the London Economic Summit, Presidents Bush and Gorbachev were able to overcome the last few obstacles on START, ending nine long years of difficult, technical negotiations. Signed in Moscow, this agreement will mark a fundamental milestone in reducing the risk of nuclear war—stabilizing the balance of strategic forces at lower levels, providing for significant reductions in the most threatening weapons and encouraging a shift toward strategic systems better suited for retaliation than for a first strike.

Our efforts to improve strategic stability will not stop here. We and the Soviets have pledged further efforts to enhance strategic stability and reduce the risk of nuclear war. We will seek agreements that improve survivability, remove incentives for a nuclear first strike and implement an appropriate relationship between strategic offenses and defenses. In particular, we will pursue Soviet agreement to permit the deployment of defenses designed to address the threat of limited ballistic missile strikes, a growing mutual concern. We are also consulting with our NATO allies on the framework that will guide the United States in future discussions with the Soviet Union on the reduction of short-range nuclear forces in Europe.

The United States has long supported international agreements designed to promote openness and freedom of navigation on the high seas. Over the past year, however, the Soviet Union has intensified efforts to restrict naval forces in ways contrary to internationally recognized rights of access. We will continue to reject such proposals. As a maritime nation, with our dependence on the sea to preserve legitimate security and commercial ties, freedom of the seas is and will remain a vital interest. We will not agree to measures that would limit the ability of our Navy to protect that interest, nor will we permit a false equation to be drawn between our Navy and regional ground-force imbalances that are inherently destabilizing. Recent events in the Gulf, Liberia, Somalia and elsewhere show that American seapower, without arbitrary limits on its force structure or operations, makes a strong contribution to global stability and mutual security.

Stemming Proliferation

As we put the main elements of European and East-West arms control into place, attention will increasingly turn to other regional and global arms control objectives. None is more urgent than stopping the global proliferation of nuclear, chemical and biological weapons, as well as the missiles to deliver them.

The Gulf crisis drove home several lessons about this challenge:

- International agreements, while essential, cannot cope with the problem alone. Iraq is a party to both the 1925 Geneva Protocol and the 1968 Nuclear Non-Proliferation Treaty (NPT). Notwithstanding its treaty obligations, Iraq has used chemical weapons and pursued nuclear ambitions.

- Export controls must be strengthened. Chemical weapons facilities in Libya and Iraq received technology and equipment from Western companies. Iraq used the deadly product of its facilities against its own people. Iraqi and several other nations' nuclear efforts and missile programs have also benefited from outside assistance.

- A successful non-proliferation strategy must address the underlying security concerns that drive the quest to obtain advanced weapons and must encompass contingency planning to deal with these weapons should prevention fail.

We are pursuing a three-tiered non-proliferation strategy: to strengthen existing arrangements; to expand the membership of multilateral regimes directed against proliferation; and to pursue new initiatives—such as the Chemical Weapons Convention and the initiative the President launched in May for the Middle East.

This latter effort reflects all the elements of our

non-proliferation strategy. It includes promising new approaches, such as a proposed set of guidelines for responsible conventional weapons transfers to the region and a proposal to freeze acquisition, production and testing of surface-to-surface missiles. It also seeks to expand the membership of the Non-Proliferation Treaty and the Biological Weapons Convention, and to strengthen the application of these and other agreements where they are already in force.

In other areas, we have already tightened export controls, streamlining export-licensing procedures while taking full account of security needs. New standards will ensure that the export of supercomputers will be subject to stringent safeguards against misuse. Criminal penalties and other sanctions against those who contribute to proliferation will be expanded.

To thwart the export of chemical and biological weapon-related materials and technology, we have expanded our own controls over precursor chemicals and proposed stringent international controls, recognizing that only multilateral measures will be truly effective in a competitive global marketplace. This multilateral approach bore fruit in the twenty-nation Australia Group of major chemical suppliers, which agreed in May to control common lists of chemical weapon precursors and equipment usable in chemical weapons manufacture. The best non-proliferation measure, of course, would be a completed Chemical Weapons Convention.

Our efforts to stem the proliferation of threatening missiles center on the multinational Missile Technology Control Regime (MTCR), strengthened last year by the inclusion of several new members. Since missile proliferation efforts will surely persist, we and our MTCR partners must improve controls, broaden membership further and reinforce the emerging international consensus against the spread of missile technology.

In the nuclear sphere, last year's review conference of the Nuclear Non-Proliferation Treaty produced a large measure of consensus that the NPT remains essential to global stability, although intransigence by a few delegations blocked unanimous agreement to a final conference declaration. The United States remains steadfast in support of the NPT and the International Atomic Energy Agency (IAEA), which provides technical assistance for civilian uses of nuclear energy while safeguarding materials essential for the development of nuclear weapons. Although trouble spots remain, progress has been made. Iraqi nuclear efforts have been set back substantially, while the UN Special Commission implementing Security Council Resolution 687 seeks dismantlement of all nuclear weapon-related activities in Iraq. Argentina and Brazil have agreed to accept IAEA safeguards on all their nuclear facilities and to take steps toward bringing into force the Treaty of Tlatelolco, which creates a Latin American nuclear-weapons-free zone. Agreement by India and Pakistan to ban attacks on each other's nuclear facilities also helped ease the tense nuclear rivalry in that part of the world.

The proliferation of advanced weapons poses an ominous challenge to global peace and stability. To meet it, we will work with our allies to address the causes of strife while curbing exports to builders of weapons of mass destruction.

Intelligence Programs

The unprecedented scope and pace of change in today's world—and the increasing number of actors now able to threaten global peace—highlight the need for reliable information and a sophisticated understanding of events and trends. The global reach of American intelligence capabilities is a unique national asset, crucial not only to our own security, but also to our leadership role in responding to international challenges.

The Soviet Union necessarily remains a major concern of U.S. policy. While changes in the Soviet Union promise hope, the turbulence of change itself demands that we monitor events and assess prospects for the future. Our monitoring of Soviet military capabilities and the effective verification of arms control treaties will remain the bedrock of any effort to build confidence and a safer world.

In a new era there are also new tasks and new priorities. Regional turmoil will place growing burdens on intelligence collection, processing and analysis. At the same time, we must track the threats posed by narcotics trafficking, terrorism and the proliferation of advanced weapons. We must also be more fully aware of international financial, trade and technology trends that could affect the security of the United States, including its economic well-being.

Sweeping political and economic changes also make for a more challenging counterintelligence environment. Warmer relations between the United States and former adversaries will open new opportunities for the intelligence services of those countries. Growing international economic competition and potential regional instabilities vastly broaden the scope of the potential intelligence threat. Our traditional openness, combined with recent changes in immigration laws and the sheer volume of information flow in the United States, affords great access to sensitive information and facilities as well as to individuals who may be targets for intelligence collection.

Economic and Security Assistance

Foreign assistance is a vital instrument of American foreign policy. Now—as we look forward to expanded cooperation with our prosperous fellow democracies, with a growing number of regional organizations and with a revitalized United Nations—we are revisiting the direction and priorities of our foreign assistance program. We will focus our efforts and resources on five major challenges:

- Promoting and consolidating democratic values: Our programs will be an increasingly valuable instrument for fostering political choice, human rights and self-determination. From Central America to South Africa to Eastern Europe, we have used our influence to advance these universal goals.
- Promoting market principles: U.S. assistance must encourage economic reform

and sustainable development. Multilaterally—through institutions like the International Monetary Fund, the World Bank, and the General Agreement on Tariffs and Trade—we foster policies that break down statist barriers to enterprise and unleash the productive forces within every society.

- Promoting peace: The bonds of collective defense can be strengthened through economic and security assistance. Such programs allow friendly states to achieve the security and stability essential for political freedom and economic growth. They are also an indispensable tool in cementing our alliance relationships—enhancing interoperability, promoting needed access and reaping goodwill.

- Protecting against transnational threats: International terrorism, narcotics, AIDS and environmental degradation threaten all peaceful nations. Our aid helps combat these dangers.

- Meeting urgent human needs. We will respond quickly and substantially to the suffering caused by natural or man-made disasters.

Managed wisely, our aid programs can play a key role in fostering a world order that comports with our fundamental values. But we must ensure that our resources are adequate, that our programs pursue well-defined goals, and that we retain the flexibility to respond to change and unforeseen requirements and opportunities. The changes we have recently proposed to the Foreign Assistance Act will eliminate obsolete and inconsistent provisions and set a solid foundation for cooperation with the Congress on a program that can respond to fast-moving events in the world as quickly as they occur. Such reform is urgently needed if our aid program is to be relevant to today's necessities.

Illicit Drugs

The international trade in drugs is a major threat to our national security. No threat does more damage to our national values and institutions, and the domestic violence generated by the trade in drugs is all too familiar. Trafficking organizations undermine the sovereign governments of our friends and weaken and distort national economies with a vast, debilitating black market and large funding requirements for enforcement, criminal justice, prevention and treatment systems. Demand reduction at home and an aggressive attack on the international drug trade are the main elements in our strategy. They must be pursued together.

During the 1990s, cocaine traffickers will likely try to develop new markets in Europe—particularly in light of the impending relaxation of border controls between EC countries—and in those nations of East Asia experiencing rapid economic growth. We can also expect increasingly energetic efforts to import cocaine and heroin into the United States, including the use of longer-range aircraft entering U.S. airspace via Canada and of drug-laden cargo containers transhipped to the United States via Europe and the Pacific. Renewed assaults on the U.S. market by increasingly sophisticated traffickers remind us of the need to also attack the drug trade at the source—its home country base of operations.

Such an effort begins with bolstering the political commitment of drug producer and transit countries to strengthen their laws, legal institutions and programs to prosecute, punish, and—where appropriate—extradite drug traffickers and money launderers. In the Andean region, where most of the world's cocaine is cultivated and refined, we seek to enhance the effectiveness of host-nation law enforcement and military activities against powerful and well entrenched trafficking organizations, and to increase public and leadership awareness of the drug threat. Our trade, aid and investment programs aim to strengthen and diversify the legitimate economies of the drug-producing Andean nations to enable them to overcome the destabilizing effects of eliminating coca and its derivatives, major sources of income. Our heroin strategy will foster cooperation with other countries, to engage their resources to dismantle their own cultivation and refining industries, and reduce demand for drugs. We will solicit the as-

Immigrants and Refugees

As a nation founded by immigrants and refugees, the United States has a strong tradition of taking in those who flee persecution and seek a better life. We open our doors annually to tens of thousands of refugees and hundreds of thousands of immigrants, welcoming both for the diversity and strength they bring the Nation. We also have a commitment to help the uprooted who are in danger or in need, a commitment demonstrated in the past several months by our role in the international effort to assist Iraqi refugees and our reaching out to Africans and others.

In 1990 the United States welcomed refugees from all regions of the world. As in the past several years, the majority came from the Soviet Union and Asia. In Vietnam, we are dismayed by continued human rights abuses. Hanoi is, however, allowing former political prisoners to emigrate. The United States resettled 14,000 former political prisoners and their family members from Vietnam in 1990 and the number will increase this year. But we cannot take in everyone. We must look to other countries to be more receptive to those in need. Nor can the United States Government fund and provide for every refugee in this country. As in the past, our private sector has an important role to play.

As noted earlier, economic hardship, political uncertainty and ethnic strife may generate large numbers of refugees in Europe. Some will be true refugees and others will be economic migrants, those who move to escape economic misery. Though international responses must differ between these two categories—to be able to protect those who flee persecution and may be in physical danger—the world's nations must be ready to respond quickly and humanely to both.

For 16 million refugees worldwide, the United States offers assistance through international programs and recognizes the critical role of nongovernmental organizations in providing care. Our budgeted refugee assistance levels have increased, and we will do our fair share. We will also meet our responsibility to search for diplomatic solutions to the problems that spawn refugee flows.

A period of turmoil and transition is often a period of dislocation. If our diplomatic efforts and our aid programs prove inadequate, the volume of refugees and migrants will be an index of our failure. The world community will need to be prepared.

· IV ·
RELATING MEANS TO ENDS:
An Economic Agenda for the 1990s

Events of the past year have reaffirmed the critical link between the strength and flexibility of the U.S. economy and our ability to achieve national objectives. Indeed, strong macroeconomic performance on the part of the United States is not only an economic objective but a prerequisite for maintaining a position of global political leadership.

Economic Challenges

Even as we now see a transformation of the global economy along lines consistent with policies we have pursued for many years, new challenges—the crisis in the Gulf and its aftermath, the political and economic transformation in Eastern Europe and potentially in the Soviet Union, the resurgence of democracy and market economies in Central and South America—have placed new demands on our management of economic policy. We must ensure that our domestic economy and our economic involvement abroad are responsive to a changing economic landscape.

Iraq's invasion of Kuwait, and actions taken by the international coalition to resist Iraqi aggression, especially tested our economic strength and our ability to help manage international economic forces. Economies around the world were affected by the volatility of oil prices and the disruption of economic ties to countries in the Gulf. Egypt, Turkey and Jordan were particularly hurt. We must continue to work to ensure the economic health of these countries as well as others that have suffered markedly from this crisis. The United States will provide leadership, but in close collaboration with major donors and creditors and with international financial institutions, particularly the International Monetary Fund and the World Bank.

As always, a dynamic domestic economy plays a critical role in helping us achieve national objectives in all spheres. Policies to control inflation, reduce the Federal deficit, promote savings, improve the labor force and encourage competitiveness and entrepreneurial initiative remain critical to our overall well-being and security. As economies expand worldwide, the economic strength of others will, of course, grow in relative terms. This is not a threat to us, but rather a success of Western policies. That said, Americans must realize that the economic strength vital to our national interests comes from investing for the future, thus putting a premium on domestic saving. Today's labor force and management, and those of tomorrow, must also be committed to quality and innovation. These are the fruits of hard work—and a prerequisite for continued global leadership.

We continue to pursue a strategy that expands and strengthens market economies around the world. This will require international efforts to open markets and expand trade; to strengthen cooperation among major industrial countries and with international financial institutions; and to apply imaginative solutions to the problems of developing countries.

Maintaining Economic Growth

Clear signs are emerging that the U.S. economy is pulling out of its brief recession but uncertainty remains over economic performance in much of the rest of the world. Therefore, macroeconomic policies in all the major countries must be designed to sustain global economic recovery with price stability. Global growth is needed in order to create a favorable economic and trade environment for reform and reconstruction in Eastern Europe and the USSR, and ensure as well the success of the democratic, market-oriented measures that have been adopted worldwide. The major countries must continue to strengthen global coordination of economic policies to achieve these aims.

Global Imbalances

While the U.S. trade deficit has continued to decline, trade imbalances with Japan and many other countries remain substantial. Reducing these imbalances remains a priority. For the United States this requires a sustained effort to reduce and ultimately eliminate budget deficits while also encouraging private savings and investment in order to preserve U.S. competitiveness. Countries with large trade surpluses bear a special responsibility for maintaining adequate growth in domestic demand and opening their markets further to imports.

Debt

The aggregate debt of developing countries was projected to reach $1.3 trillion in 1990, according to the World Bank. Inappropriate domestic policies in debtor countries—overvalued exchange rates, large budget deficits, investment in inefficient public enterprises and restrictions on trade and investment—were major causes of this debt accumulation and contributed to capital flight. External shocks, high international interest rates and recession in the 1980s also hurt. Recently this burden has been exacerbated by the economic dislocations and fluctuations in energy prices resulting from the Gulf crisis.

In March 1989, the United States proposed a new international debt strategy that advanced voluntary reduction of commercial bank debt and debt service to help restore debtor financial health and pave the way for new commercial bank lending. Implementation of a strong economic reform program supported by the IMF and World Bank is a prerequisite. So far, Mexico, Costa Rica, Nigeria, the Philippines, Venezuela, Morocco, Uruguay and Chile have negotiated agreements under these proposals. Others are undertaking reforms to obtain such support.

Creditor governments have also made substantial contributions to relief through rescheduling of official bilateral debt and have recently offered new treatment for the official debt of lower middle income countries, as mandated by last year's Houston Economic Summit, and for Poland and Egypt. The Enterprise for the Americas Initiative also promotes growth in Latin America by emphasizing official debt reduction and investment reform.

Trade

Countries accept as natural that trade and investment should flow freely within national boundaries or within special regional groupings in order to improve economic and social welfare. Internationally, this concept has met varying degrees of acceptance. Countries have protected certain sectors for national security, economic, industrial or social reasons.

For the last 50 years, significant efforts have been undertaken, primarily through the General Agreement on Tariffs and Trade (GATT), to expand trade among all nations by opening markets and resolving trade disputes. The latest and most ambitious effort has been the Uruguay Round of Multilateral Trade Negotiations, begun in 1986. The Uruguay Round is distinguished from previous efforts by the intention of GATT members to extend GATT rules to areas such as agriculture, services, investment, the protection of intellectual property and textiles. At the Houston Economic Summit in 1990, the United States, Canada, Japan, France, Germany, Italy, the United Kingdom, and the European Community committed to removing trade barriers in these politically difficult areas. The wise action of Congress in extending "fast track" procedures for trade agreements is evidence of America's commitment to responsible leadership.

The promise of the Uruguay Round has yet to be fulfilled, however, primarily because of strong differences over the scope and pace of efforts to dismantle the enormous barriers to trade in agricultural goods. Given the interdependence of modern economies, and the need to expand trading opportunities for emerging democracies and other developing countries, it is important that the Round be brought to a successful conclusion. This is a test of the ability and willingness of all countries to rise to the challenges of a new world order and will require compromise on all sides. The United States will do its part. A successful Round will not end bilateral trade disputes but it will enable countries to resolve them in a multilateral context and on the basis of internationally agreed rules.

The United States will continue its efforts to expand trade further. We are working with Japan under the Structural Impediments Initiative to lower trade barriers. As noted earlier, we are building on the successful U.S.-Canada Free Trade Agreement by undertaking discussions with Mexico and Canada which we expect will lead to a trilateral free trade agreement linking all three economies. The Enterprise for the Americas Initiative and preferential trade programs for the Caribbean basin and the Andean region will also foster trade liberalization.

Technology

The interrelationship of economic and military strength has never been stronger. Both are affected by the way technology transfer is handled, particularly with respect to export controls. Balances must be struck. Loss of technological leadership can undermine military readiness and strength. Not participating freely in worldwide markets constrains economic growth. Recent changes to our strategic trade policies reflect a new balance between these competing factors.

In cooperation with our Western partners in the Coordinating Committee for Multilateral Export Controls (COCOM), we have completely overhauled export controls, reducing them to a core list of only the most strategically significant goods and technologies. This action reflects the emergence of democratic governments in Eastern Europe as well as a reduced military threat to the United States and our allies from a dissolved Warsaw Pact and a Soviet army that is withdrawing. The result has been a two-thirds reduction in the licenses that industry is required to obtain prior to exporting.

Treating the new democracies of Central and Eastern Europe differently from the Soviet Union, we and our COCOM partners have adopted a wide-ranging special procedure for Poland, Hungary and Czechoslovakia that ensures that controlled technology imports are used for purely civilian applications. We look forward to the day when we can remove these countries completely from the list of proscribed destinations. We have a strong interest in promoting the growth of free markets in democratic societies. At the same time we must be sure that the easing of COCOM controls does not result in the proliferation of dangerous technologies to other areas like the Middle East. For that reason, we have—in close cooperation with other supplier nations—significantly improved controls on technologies useful in developing nuclear, chemical and biological weapons and the missiles to deliver them.

Energy

Secure, ample, diversified and clean supplies of energy are essential to our national economic prosperity and security. For the foreseeable future, oil will remain a vital element in our energy mix. For geological and economic reasons, U.S. oil imports are likely to increase in coming years. The rate of increase, however, could be reduced by improving the efficiency with which oil is used in the economy and by substituting alternative fuels.

Security of oil supplies is enhanced by a supportive foreign policy and appropriate military capabilities. We will work to improve understanding among key participants in the oil industry of the basic fundamentals of the oil market. We will also maintain our capability to respond to requests to protect vital oil facilities, on land or at sea, while working to resolve the underlying political, social and economic tensions that could threaten the free flow of oil.

The stability of the Gulf region, which contains two-thirds of the world's known oil reserves, is of fundamental concern to us. Political and military turbulence in the region has a direct impact on our economy, largely through higher oil prices and potential supply disruptions. Diversification of both productive and spare capacity is important to providing a cushion to the oil market. Increased production, in an environmentally sound manner, from other areas would also contribute to the security of oil supplies.

Because energy markets—particularly the oil market—are global, our energy security requires close cooperation among energy consumers. The aftermath of Iraq's invasion of Kuwait demonstrates the need to improve strategic stock levels within oil-consuming countries and the value of international cooperation to help mitigate damage brought about by sudden, serious disruptions of supply. The United States should develop creative mechanisms to fill its Strategic Petroleum Reserve to the statutorily required one billion barrels, consistent with sound budgetary practices and avoiding an unnecessary burden on the oil market.

Our use of oil is the key source of our vulnerability to world oil supply disruption. To reduce this vulnerability, we must work to both reduce oil consumption and to use oil more efficiently. The efficient use of energy in all sectors of our economy is of particular importance. We must intensify the development of alternative sources of energy (nuclear, natural gas, coal and renewables) and support aggressive research and development of advanced energy technologies to provide the clean, affordable, reliable energy supplies we will need in the mid-21st century.

To meet pressing environmental concerns, we must limit the harmful effects of energy production, transportation and use. The increased, safe use of nuclear power, for example, can significantly reduce greenhouse gas emissions.

The Environment

We must manage the Earth's natural resources in ways that protect the potential for growth and opportunity for present and future generations. The experience of the past half-century has taught that democratic political institutions and free market economies enhance human well-being. But even as we experience political and economic success, we cannot ignore the costs that growth, unguided by wisdom, can impose on our natural environment. A healthy economy and a healthy environment go hand-in-hand. Solutions must be found that protect our environment while allowing for the economic development needed to improve the living standards of a growing world population.

Global environmental concerns include such diverse but interrelated issues as stratospheric ozone depletion, climate change, food security, water supply, deforestation, biodiversity and treatment of wastes. A common ingredient in each is that they respect no international boundaries. The stress from these environmental challenges is already contributing to political conflict. Recognizing a shared responsibility for global stewardship is a necessary step for global progress. Our partners will find the United States a ready and active participant in this effort.

Space

The time has come to look beyond brief space encounters and to commit to a future in which Americans and citizens of all nations live and work in space. We have developed a plan to make this vision a reality and the National Space Council, under Vice President Quayle, is charged with bringing coherence, continuity and commitment to our efforts. We have made solid progress in the five key elements of our space strategy:

- Developing our space launch capability as a national resource: This infrastructure will be to the 21st century what the great highway and dam projects were to the 20th. Reliable space launchers will provide the "highway" to space and the solar system in the next century.

- Expanding human presence and activity beyond earth orbit and into the Solar System: We are well underway with unmanned exploration of the Solar System. Magellan, Viking and Voyager have been spectacular successes, Galileo is on its way to Jupiter, Ulysses has launched on its wide-ranging orbit of the sun and soon we will begin missions to Saturn and the Asteroid Belt. The Space Exploration Initiative will build on the successes and expertise developed in the Apollo, Skylab, Space Shuttle and eventually the

Space Station Freedom programs, ultimately establishing permanent human settlements on the Moon and putting humans on Mars.

- Obtaining scientific, technological and economic benefits and improving the quality of life on earth: Communications satellites already link people around the globe; their contribution to the free flow of information and ideas played a part in the Revolution of '89. We also use space systems to verify arms control treaties. But the potential of space to improve life on earth has barely been tapped. A very promising application is in the area of the environment—monitoring and helping to understand the process of ecological change, and holding significant promise for new sources of energy, material and products.

- Capitalizing on the unique environment of space to foster economic well-being: Private investment in space will create jobs, boost the economy and strengthen our scientific, engineering and industrial base. New commercial markets will be created, and existing industries will become stronger and more competitive in the world marketplace. The recently approved commercial launch policy is a first step in this process.

- Ensuring the freedom of space for exploration and development: There are now some ten significant spacefaring nations, with others on the way. Space will become in the future what oceans have always been—highways to discovery and commerce. But as with sea lanes, space lanes can be closed and can even be used as springboards for attack. We must ensure the freedom to use space for exploration and development, for ourselves and all nations.

Assured access to space requires a healthy military space program. We must be able to monitor events in space, warn of threats and intervene to protect important space assets. This protection may take the form of passive measures to enhance the survivability of critical systems. We must also have the option of active defense systems, including an anti-satellite system, to stop an aggressor before he can use a space system to threaten objects or people in or from space.

·V·
RELATING MEANS TO ENDS:
A Defense Agenda for the 1990s

As the war to liberate Kuwait clearly showed, the essential demands on our military forces—to deter conflict whenever possible but to prevail in those that do arise—are certain to endure. Nonetheless, the specific challenges facing our military in the 1990s and beyond will be different from those that have dominated our thinking for the past 40 years.

In a world less driven by an immediate, massive threat to Europe or the danger of global war, the need to support a smaller but still crucial forward presence and to deal with regional contingencies—including possibly a limited, conventional threat to Europe—will shape how we organize, equip, train, deploy and employ our active and reserve forces. We must also have the ability to reconstitute forces, if necessary, to counter any resurgent global threat.

As the war in the Gulf made clear, the easing of the Soviet threat does not mean an end to all hazards. As we seek to build a new world order in the aftermath of the Cold War, we will likely discover that the enemy we face is less an expansionist communism than it is instability itself.

And, in the face of multiple and varied threats to stability, we will increasingly find our military strength a source of reassurance and a foundation for security, regionally and globally.

In the face of competing fiscal demands and a changing but still dangerous world, we have developed a new defense strategy that provides the conceptual framework for our future forces. This new strategy will guide our deliberate reductions to no more than the forces we need to defend our interests and meet our global responsibilities. It will also guide our restructuring so that our remaining forces are appropriate to the challenges of a new era. The four fundamental demands of a new era are already clear: to ensure strategic deterrence, to exercise forward presence in key areas, to respond effectively to crises and to retain the national capacity to reconstitute forces should this ever be needed.

Nuclear Deterrence

Deterrence will indeed be enhanced as a result of the START Treaty and U.S. force modernization efforts can go forward with greater knowledge and predictability about future Soviet forces. Nevertheless, even with the Treaty, Soviet nuclear capabilities will remain substantial. Despite economic and political difficulties, the Soviet Union continues its modernization of strategic forces. Even in a new era, deterring nuclear attack remains the number one defense priority of the United States.

Strategic Nuclear Forces

The modernization of our Triad of land-based missiles, strategic bombers and submarine-launched missiles will be vital to the effectiveness of our deterrent in the next century. We need to complete the Trident submarine program with the eighteen boats and modern missiles necessary to ensure a survivable force. The B-2 strategic bomber must be deployed so that the flexibility traditionally provided by the bomber force will be available in the future. The B-2 will also firmly plant our aerospace industry in a new era of low-observable technology and the bomber itself will have unique value across the spectrum of conflict. Finally, we must continue the development of land-based, mobile ICBMs in order to keep our deployment options open.

Our command, control and communications capabilities are critical to nuclear deterrence and to ensuring the survivability of our constitutional government under all circumstances of attack. Our civil defense program is still needed to deal with the consequences of an attack, while also providing important capabilities to respond to natural and man-made catastrophes.

The safety, security, control and effectiveness of United States nuclear weapon systems are also of paramount importance. We are incorporating the most modern safety and control features into our deterrent stockpile as rapidly as practicable and developing new safety technologies for future weapons. Older weapons that lack the most modern safety features are being replaced or retired.

Testing of nuclear weapons plays a key part in assuring the safety and effectiveness of our deterrent forces. While we test only as much as is required for national security purposes, testing is essential to ensure the reliability and effectiveness of our weapons, to identify any safety issues and to prove any corrective measures. A halt to nuclear testing would not eliminate weapons or increase security, but it would erode confidence in our deterrent and severely restrict our ability to make improvements, especially in nuclear safety.

Just as our weapons must be safe, the facilities that produce them must be safe, efficient, economical, and environmentally sound. Our current facilities are being renovated and brought up to modern standards. At the same time we are moving forward to consolidate and reconfigure the current large and older complex, looking toward one that will be smaller, more flexible and more efficient. Our production complex must be able to respond to potential needs ranging from accelerated production to accelerated retirement of weapons, depending on the security environment in the years ahead.

We must also recognize that the deterrence issues of a new era are now at hand. Despite the threat still posed by the existence of Soviet nuclear weapons, the likelihood of their deliberate use by the Soviet state is declining and the scenario which we frequently projected as the precursor of their use—massive war in Europe—is less likely than at any other time since World War II. These developments affect questions of nuclear targeting, the alert status and operational procedures of our forces and ultimately the type and number of weapons sufficient to ensure our safety and that of our allies. We have already begun to make adjustments to our nuclear forces and to the policies that guide them in recognition of the disintegration of the Warsaw Pact and changes in the Soviet Union itself. Beyond this, while we have traditionally focused on deterring a unitary, rational actor applying a relatively knowable calculus of potential costs and gains, our thinking must now encompass potential instabilities within states as well as the potential threat from states or leaders who might perceive they have little to lose in employing weapons of mass destruction.

Non-Strategic Nuclear Forces

Below the level of strategic forces, we have traditionally maintained other nuclear forces for a variety of purposes. They have highlighted our resolve and have helped to link conventional defense to the broader strategic nuclear guarantee of the United States. This has helped remove incentives that otherwise might have accelerated nuclear proliferation. These systems have also served to deter an enemy's use of such weapons and they have contributed to the deterrence of conventional attack. These needs persist.

In Europe, we and our allies have always sought the lowest number and most stable types of weapons needed to prevent war. Indeed, NATO has unilaterally reduced thousands of nuclear weapons over the past decade, in addition to the elimination of an entire class of U.S. and Soviet weapons as called for in the Treaty on Intermediate Range Nuclear Forces. Changes in Europe have now allowed us to forgo plans to modernize our LANCE missiles and nuclear artillery shells and we will work to implement the commitments of the London Declaration with respect to short-range nuclear weapons currently deployed in Europe.

Even with the dramatic changes we see in Europe, however, non-strategic nuclear weapons remain integral to our strategy of deterrence. They make NATO's resolve unmistakably clear and help prevent war by ensuring that there are no circumstances in which a nuclear response to military action might be discounted. In practical terms, this means greater reliance on aircraft armed with modern weapons. As the principal means by which Alliance members share nuclear risks and burdens, these aircraft and their weapons must be based in Europe. Such a posture is not designed to threaten any European state but to provide a secure deterrent in the face of unforeseen circumstances.

Missile Defenses

Flexible response and deterrence through the threat of retaliation have preserved the security of the United States and its allies for decades. In the early 1980s, we began the Strategic Defense Initiative in the face of an unconstrained Soviet ballistic-missile program and a significant Soviet commitment to strategic defenses. SDI was intended to shift deterrence to a safer, more stable basis as effective strategic defenses would diminish the confidence of an adversary in his ability to execute a successful attack.

Notwithstanding the continued modernization of Soviet offensive forces and the pursuit of more effective strategic defenses, the positive changes in our relationship with the Soviet Union and the fundamental changes in Eastern Europe have markedly reduced the danger of a war in Europe that could escalate to the strategic nuclear level. At the same time, the threat posed by global ballistic-missile proliferation and by an accidental or unauthorized launch resulting from political turmoil has grown considerably. Thus, the United States, our forces, and our allies and friends face a continued and even growing threat from ballistic missiles.

In response to these trends, we have redirected

SDI to pursue a system providing Global Protection Against Limited Strikes (GPALS). With adequate funding, it will be possible to begin to deploy systems that will better protect our troops in the field from ballistic-missile attack by the mid-1990s and that will protect the United States itself from such attacks by the turn of the century. GPALS is designed to provide protection against a ballistic missile launched from anywhere against a target anywhere in the world. The system will be based on technologies which SDI has pioneered, but would be both smaller and less expensive than the initial deployment originally projected for SDI.

GPALS offers many potential advantages: the United States would be protected against limited strikes by ballistic missiles; our forward-deployed forces would be better defended against missile attacks; and our allies, many of whom lie on the edge of troubled areas, could also be better protected. The record of the PATRIOT against Iraqi SCUDs highlights the great potential for defenses against ballistic missiles, the critical role of missile defenses and the need to improve such defenses further.

GPALS could also provide incentives against further proliferation of ballistic missiles. If these missiles did not hold the potential to cause certain and immediate damage, nations might be less likely to go to such great lengths to acquire them. Access to U.S. assistance in defenses may also provide an incentive for countries not to seek ballistic missiles or weapons of mass destruction.

Forward Presence

Maintaining a positive influence in distant regions requires that we demonstrate our engagement. The forward presence of our military forces often provides the essential glue in important alliance relationships and signals that our commitments are backed by tangible actions. Our presence can deter aggression, preserve regional balances, deflect arms races and prevent the power vacuums that invite conflict. While our forward deployments will be reduced in the future, the prudent forward basing of forces and the prepositioning of equipment reduce the burden of projecting power from the continental United States. Indeed, certain regions—like Europe and East Asia—represent such compelling interests to the United States that they will demand the permanent deployment of some U.S. forces for as long as they are needed and welcomed by our allies as part of a common effort. But even in these regions, the size of our forward deployments can be smaller as the threat diminishes and the defense capabilities of our allies improve. In other regions our presence, while important, can take less permanent forms.

Across the Atlantic: Europe and the Middle East

In Europe, Soviet reductions and the dissolution of the Warsaw Pact allow us to scale back our presence to a smaller, but still significant, contribution to NATO's overall force levels. This presence will include the equivalent of a robust army corps, with a corps headquarters, associated corps units, and two ground force divisions supplemented by several air wings, appropriate naval forces, and sufficient infrastructure to support a return of additional forces. Such a force will preserve the operational, not just symbolic, significance of our presence.

As called for in July at the London NATO Summit, we will work with our allies to make our forces in Europe more flexible and mobile and more fully integrated into multinational formations. NATO will establish a multinational Rapid Reaction Corps to respond to crises and we expect Alliance forces, including those of the United States, to be organized into multinational corps that would function in peacetime, and not just be contingent structures activated in a crisis. We will also exploit the prospect of longer warning time in the event of a major crisis by backing up our deployed forces with the ability to reinforce them with active and reserve units from the United States, supported by the ability to reconstitute larger forces over time should the need arise.

The aftermath of the crisis in the Gulf portends a need for some measure of continuing presence in that region consistent with the desires and needs of our friends. While the United States will not maintain a permanent ground presence, we are committed to the region's security. We will work with our friends to bolster their confidence and security through such measures as exercises, prepositioning of heavy equipment and an enhanced naval presence. Our vital national interests depend on a stable and secure Gulf.

Across the Pacific

Our enduring interests in East Asia and the Pacific also demand forces sufficient to meet our responsibilities and to sustain our long-term relationships with friends and allies. While East Asia has been considerably less affected by the Revolution of '89 than Europe, the growing strength and self-reliance of our friends in the region permit some reduction in our presence.

A phased approach, responding to global and regional events, is the soundest. We have announced our intent to adjust military personnel levels in the Philippines, the Republic of Korea and Japan. This phase is designed to thin out existing force structure and reshape our security relationships. Before this phase ends in December 1992, over 15,000 U.S. personnel will be withdrawn. Later phases will reduce and reorganize our force structure further, as circumstances permit.

Korea represents the area of greatest potential danger, and reductions there must be carefully measured against North Korean actions. However, we have judged that the growing strength of our Korean allies permits us to reduce our presence and begin to move toward a security partnership in which the Korean armed forces assume the leading role. We are also encouraged by the progress of the Japanese Government in rounding out its own self-defense capabilities.

The Rest of the World

In other regions, as the need for our presence persists, we will increasingly rely on periodic visits, training missions, access agreements, prepositioned equipment, exercises, combined planning and security and humanitarian assistance to sustain the sense of common interest and cooperation on which we would rely in deploying and employing our military forces. As the Gulf crisis clearly showed, our strategy is increasingly dependent on the support of regional friends and allies. In fact—during crises—the cooperation and support of those local states most directly threatened will be critical factors in determining our own course of action.

Crisis Response

Despite our best efforts to deter conflict, we must be prepared for our interests to be challenged with force, often with little or no warning. The Gulf crisis was ample evidence that such challenges will not always be small or easily resolved. Because regional crises are the predominant military threat we will face in the future, their demands—along with our forward presence requirements—will be the primary determinant of the size and structure of our future forces.

The regional contingencies we could face are many and varied. We must be prepared for differences in terrain, climate and the nature of threatening forces, as well as for differing levels of support from host nations or others. We must also be able to respond quickly and effectively to adversaries who may possess cruise missiles, modern air defenses, chemical weapons, ballistic missiles and even large armor formations. Although our forward deployed forces speed our ability to respond to threats in areas like the Pacific or Europe, there are other regions where threats, while likely to be less formidable, may prove no less urgent.

Mobility

In this new era, therefore, the ability to project our power will underpin our strategy more than ever. We must be able to deploy substantial forces and sustain them in parts of the world where prepositioning of equipment will not always be feasible, where adequate bases may not be available (at least before a crisis) and where there is a less developed industrial base and infrastructure to support our forces once they have arrived. Our strategy demands we be able to move men and materiel to the scene of a crisis at a pace and in numbers sufficient to field an overwhelming force. The 100-hour success of our ground forces in the war to liberate Kuwait was stunning, but we should not allow it to obscure the fact that we required six months to deploy these forces. As our overall force levels draw down and our forward-deployed forces shrink, we must sustain and expand our investment in airlift, sealift and—where possible—prepositioning. We must also ensure unimpeded transit of the air and sea lanes and access to space through maritime and aerospace superiority. Our security assistance must, among other things, enhance the ability of other nations to facilitate our deployments. And, over the longer term, we must challenge our technology to develop forces that are lethal but more readily deployable and more easily sustained than today's.

Readiness and Our Guard and Reserve Forces

For almost two decades, our Total Force Policy has placed a substantial portion of our military manpower in high-quality, well-trained, well-equipped and early-mobilizing Guard and Reserve units. Compared to maintaining such a force in the active component, this was a cost-effective strategy, a prudent response to an international security environment where the predominant threat was major conflict in Europe or global war with the Soviets, with warning of such a conflict measured in weeks or even days.

That environment has been transformed. Today we must reshape our Guard and Reserve forces so that they can continue their important contributions in new circumstances. While we still face the possibility of sudden conflict in many of the regional contingencies that could concern us, these threats—despite their danger—will be on a smaller scale than the threat formerly posed by the Soviets and their Warsaw Pact allies. This will allow a smaller force overall, but those units oriented towards short-warning, regional contingencies must be kept at high readiness.

Over time we will move to a Total Force that permits us to respond initially to any regional contingency with units—combat and support—drawn wholly from the active component, except for a limited number of support and mobility assets. Since many support functions can be more economically maintained in the reserve component, we will still rely on reserve support units in any extended confrontation. The primary focus of reserve combat units will be to supplement active units in any especially large or protracted deployment. To hedge against a future need for expanded forces to deal with a renewed global confrontation, which—though possible—is less likely and clearly less immediate than previously calculated, some reserve combat units will be retained in cadre status.

This approach will allow us to maintain a Total Force appropriate for the strategic and fiscal demands of a new era: a smaller, more self-contained and very ready active force able to respond quickly to emerging threats; and a reduced but still essential reserve component with emphasis on supporting and sustaining active combat forces, and—in particularly large or prolonged regional contingencies—providing latent combat capability that can be made ready when needed.

Even as we restructure for a new era, we will continue to place a premium on the quality of our military personnel, the backbone of any effective fighting force. True military power is measured by the professional skills and dedication of our young men and women. In six weeks and 100 decisive hours, today's military proved it is the most skilled and effective fighting force this Nation has ever possessed. As we make the adjustments appropriate to a new environment, we will preserve this precious resource.

Reconstitution

Beyond the crisis response capabilities provided by active and reserve forces, we must have the ability to generate wholly new forces should the need arise. Although we are hopeful for the future, history teaches us caution. The 20th century has seen rapid shifts in the geopolitical climate, and technology has repeatedly transformed the battlefield. The ability to reconstitute is what allows us safely and selectively to scale back and restructure our forces in-being.

This difficult task will require us to invest in hedging options whose future dividends may not always be measurable now. It will require careful attention to the vital elements of our military potential: the industrial base, science and technology, and manpower. These elements were easily accommodated in an era when we had to maintain large standing forces, when we routinely invested heavily in defense R&D and when new items of equipment were broadly and extensively produced. We will now have to work much more deliberately to preserve them.

The standard by which we should measure our efforts is the response time that our warning processes would provide us of a return to previous levels of confrontation in Europe or in the world at large. We and our allies must be able to reconstitute a credible defense faster than any potential opponent can generate an overwhelming offense.

Manpower

Reconstitution obviously includes manpower. Relatively large numbers of personnel, trained in basic military skills, can be raised in one to two years. But skilled, seasoned leaders—high-quality senior NCOs and officers—require many years to develop and we must preserve this critical nucleus to lead an expanding military force. This must be reflected in how we man active, reserve and cadre units over the long term.

Defense Technology

Another challenge will be to maintain our edge in defense technology, even as we reduce our forces. Technology has historically been a comparative advantage for American forces, and we have often relied on it to overcome numerical disparities and to reduce the risk to American lives.

Our technological edge in key areas of warfare will be even more important at lower levels of forces and funding, and in the complex political and military environment in which our forces will operate. But maintaining this margin will become increasingly difficult as access to advanced weaponry spreads and as our defense industry shrinks. Even in regional contingencies it will not be uncommon for our forces to face high-technology weapons in the hands of adversaries. This spread of advanced systems will surely erode the deterrent value of our own—and our competitive edge in warfare—unless we act decisively to maintain technological superiority.

We will, of course, have to decide which technologies we want to advance and how we will pursue them. Our focus should be on promising, high-leverage areas, especially those that play to our comparative advantages and exploit the weaknesses of potential adversaries, whoever and wherever they may be. Stealth, space-based systems, sensors, precision weapons, advanced training technologies—all these proved themselves in the Gulf, yet when these programs (and others) were begun, no one foresaw their use against Iraq. Our investment strategies must hedge against the unknown, giving future Presidents the flexibility that such capabilities provide.

We must be able to move promising research through development to rapid fielding when changes in the international environment so require. The "generation leaps" in technology and fielded systems that some have suggested may not be possible. We will have to build some systems, as the early production effort is a vital component of technology development. Production, even in limited numbers, will also facilitate the development of innovative doctrine and organizational structures to make full use of the new technologies we field. In an era of tight fiscal constraints, our development efforts must also strive to make our weapons less expensive as well as more effective.

In the competition for scarce resources, emphasis on technology development—to pursue those new capabilities that may be most decisive in the longer term—may mean accepting some continued risk in the near term. But accepting such risk may well be prudent in a period of reduced East-West tensions.

The Industrial Base

Providing and sustaining modern equipment to support a rapid expansion of the armed forces is an equally difficult proposition. We will need a production base to produce new systems and a maintenance and repair base to support them. These requirements pose unique problems, as reduced defense budgets are shrinking the defense industrial sector overall. As we make procurement and investment decisions, we will have to place a value on the assured supply and timely delivery of defense materials in time of crisis.

In the near term, some of these problems can be ameliorated by retaining and storing equipment from units being deactivated. Over the longer term, however, as stored equipment becomes obsolete, the issue becomes our capability to expand production or use alternative sources of supply. We will need the capacity for industrial surge, accelerating orders that are already in the pipeline. We will also have to plan for production from new or alternative industrial capacity. It may also be possible to reduce unneeded military specifications to make greater use of items that can be created by the commercial production base. Above all, we must continue to involve the creative resources of our national economy and ensure that corporations continue to have incentives to engage in innovative defense work.

A Smaller and Restructured Force

Our future military will be smaller. Assuming there are no unforeseen, worrisome trends in the security environment, by mid-decade our force can be some 25 percent smaller than the force we maintained in the last days of the Cold War. The changes we have seen in the overall international environment have made this smaller force possible, and the increasing demands on our resources to preserve the other elements of our national strength have made it necessary.

Minimum Essential Military Forces—The Base Force

Yet these planned reductions will cut our forces to a minimally acceptable level—to a Base Force below which further reductions would not be prudent. These minimum forces represent our national security insurance policy and consist of four basic force packages: *Strategic Forces, Atlantic Forces, Pacific Forces* and *Contingency Forces.*

Our *Strategic Forces* continue to meet the enduring demands of nuclear deterrence and defense. The conventional force packages provide forces for forward presence as well as the ability to respond to crises. Our *Atlantic Forces* will be postured and trained for the heavy threats characteristic of Europe and Southwest Asia and must be modern and lethal enough to deal with these threats. *Pacific Forces* will be structured for an essentially maritime theater, placing a premium on naval capabilities, backed by the essential air and ground forces for enduring deterrence and immediate crisis response. U.S.-based reinforcements will be lighter than those we envisage for the Atlantic, as befits the potential contingencies in the Pacific. *Contingency Forces* will include the Army's light and airborne units, Marine expeditionary brigades, special operations forces and selected air and naval assets. They will be largely based in the United States and—since they must be able to respond to spontaneous and unpredictable crises—they will largely be in the active component. At times, the quick deployment of such a force in itself may be enough to head off confrontation. At other times, we may need actually to employ this force to deal with insurgencies, conduct anti-drug or anti-terrorist operations, evacuate non-combatants or—as we did in Desert Shield—be the first into action while heavier forces are alerted and moved.

The reductions projected by the mid-1990s are dramatic. It will be important to manage their pace rationally and responsibly. We must accommodate the actions taken in support of Desert Storm and Desert Shield and we must be attentive to the professional skills of the armed forces that have been built up over the past decade—and which, as the war made clear, remain vital to our national security. But now that the war has been won, and as long as no unanticipated ominous trends emerge, we will get back on the spending path agreed to before hostilities began. Highly effective military forces can be supported within the levels agreed to by Congress in the 1990 Budget Agreement if we can end unneeded programs, consolidate bases, streamline procedures and adjust overall manpower levels without arbitrary restrictions.

·VI·
TOWARD THE 21ST CENTURY

The 20th century has taught us that security is indivisible. The safety, freedom and well-being of one people cannot be separated from the safety, freedom and well-being of all. Recently, the Gulf crisis strengthened this sense of international community. Many of the underlying forces now at work in the world are tending to draw that global community even closer together. Technology, especially the explosion of communication and information, has accelerated the pace of human contact. The growing acceptance of the democratic ideal—evidenced in the erosion of totalitarianism and the expansion of basic human freedoms—has also brought the world closer together. The expansion of commerce and the growing acceptance of market principles have accelerated the movement toward interdependence and the integration of economies. Even the threats posed by the proliferation of weapons of enormous destructiveness have begun to draw the community of nations together in common concern.

As we move toward the 21st century, this interdependence of peoples will grow and will continue to demand responsible American leadership. Guided by the values that have inspired and nurtured our democracy at home, we will work for a new world in which peace, security and cooperation finally replace the confrontation of the Cold War, and overcome the kind of threat represented by Iraq's aggression.

Developments in the Soviet Union and elsewhere have set in motion a change in the strategic landscape as dramatic as that which the Nation experienced when Soviet policy first forced the Cold War upon us. The great threat to global peace has ebbed and we now see a Soviet state and society struggling to overcome severe internal crisis. Notwithstanding the uncertainties about the future course of the Soviet Union, that state's willingness—indeed, in many ways, its ability—to project power beyond its borders has been dramatically reduced for the foreseeable future. Our strategy for this new era recognizes the opportunities and challenges before us, and includes among its principles:

- reinforcing the moral ties that hold our alliances together, even as perceptions of a common security threat change;

- encouraging the constructive evolution of the Soviet Union, recognizing the limits of our influence and the continuing power of Soviet military forces;

- supporting the independence and vitality of the new Eastern European democracies even as we deal with the uncertainties of the Soviet future;

- championing the principles of political and economic freedom as the surest guarantors of human progress and happiness, as well as global peace;

- working with others in the global community to resolve regional disputes and stem the proliferation of advanced weapons;

- cooperating with the Soviet Union and others in achieving arms control agreements that promote security and stability;

- reducing our defense burden as appropriate, while restructuring our forces for new challenges;

- tending more carefully to our own economic competitiveness as the foundation of our long-term strength; and

- addressing the new global agenda of refugee flows, drug abuse and environmental degradation.

We are a rich and powerful nation, and the elements of our power will remain formidable. But our wealth and our strength are not without limits. We must balance our commitments with our means and, above all, we must wisely choose *now* which elements of our strength will best serve our needs in the *future*. This is the challenge of strategy.

In this country we make such choices for peace just as we make the awful choices of war—as a democracy. When President and Congress work together to build an effective security posture and policy—as was done in the 1980s—we are successful. In the Gulf, our armed forces benefited from the legacy of investment decisions, technological innovations, and strategic planning that came in the decade before. Today's planning decisions will determine whether we are well or ill prepared for the contingencies that will confront us in the future.

This is a heavy responsibility, shared between the President and Congress. We owe our servicemen and women not only the best equipment, but also a coherent strategy and posture geared to new realities. This coherence can only come from a partnership between the Branches. Divided, we will invite disasters. United, we can overcome any challenge.

In the Gulf, the dictator guessed wrong when he doubted America's unity and will. The extraordinary unity we showed as a Nation in the Gulf assured that we would prevail. It also sent the message loud and clear that America is prepared for the challenges of the future, committed and engaged in the world, as a reliable ally, friend and leader.